WHAT'S THE WEATHER?

IT'S

WINDY!

Written by
Azra Limbada

BookLife PUBLISHING

King's Lynn
Norfolk, PE30 4LS

Printed in Malaysia.

A catalogue record for this book is available from the British Library.

ISBN: 978-1-83927-195-3

Written by:
Azra Limbada

Edited by:
William Anthony

Designed by:
Drue Rintoul &
Danielle Webster-Jones

PHOTO CREDITS

*All images are courtesy of Shutterstock.com, unless otherwise specified. With thanks to Getty Images, Thinkstock Photo and iStockphoto.
Front Cover – Toms Auzins, TippaPatt, Olga_Kuzmina, AlexLinck, S Curtis. Character throughout – yusufdemirci.
4 – Rushvol. 5 – traXX. 6 – Incomible. 7 – YanLev, STUDIO GRAND WEB. 8–9 – Merggy, pixfix, Oksana Shufrych. 10 – 11 – Merggy, AlexTanya, Guntsoophack Yuktahnon. 12–13 – Romrodphoto, PR Image Factory. 14–15 – NIKS ADS, Sergey Novikov. 16–17 – lovelyday12, Amelia Fox, designer_an. 18 – FotoKina. 19 – Irina Kozorog. 20 – DanGui, Minerva Studio. 21 – FotoKina. 22 – Dejan-Milosavljevic. 23 – SunflowerMomma.*

CONTENTS

Words that look like this can be found in the glossary on page 24.

WHAT CAN YOU SEE?

Take a look outside. What can you see?

Are the leaves blowing in the wind or is the Sun shining brightly?

Weather is what you can see in the sky and feel in the air outside. There are lots of types of weather, such as rain, snow, sunshine and wind.

SEASONS

In most countries, there are four seasons in every year. They are called spring, summer, autumn and winter. Each season has different kinds of weather.

Some types of weather can make us feel very cold and other types of weather can make us feel very warm.

IT'S WINDY!

Wind is air that moves from one place to another. It can be gentle or strong. Sometimes, wind moves very quickly.

These children are playing with a parachute by throwing it up in the wind.

It is often windy when the weather is cold, but we can also have warm winds in the summer.

WHERE DOES WIND COME FROM?

Clouds are made when warm air rises into the sky and then gets colder.

When air gets warm, it rises up. Colder air from all around rushes in to fill the gap it left. This rushing air is wind.

Warm air rises.

There are lots of different types of wind. A strong wind can even blow you off your feet!

A **breeze** can help cool you down on a hot day!

Colder air rushes to fill the gap.

WHAT TO WEAR

In winter, the wind may make you feel very cold. It is a good idea to wrap up warm in your coat, hat, gloves and scarf.

When the temperature is warm, you might want to wear light clothes that will help you stay cool if there is no wind.

A fan can cool you down by blowing air over you, just like a breeze would.

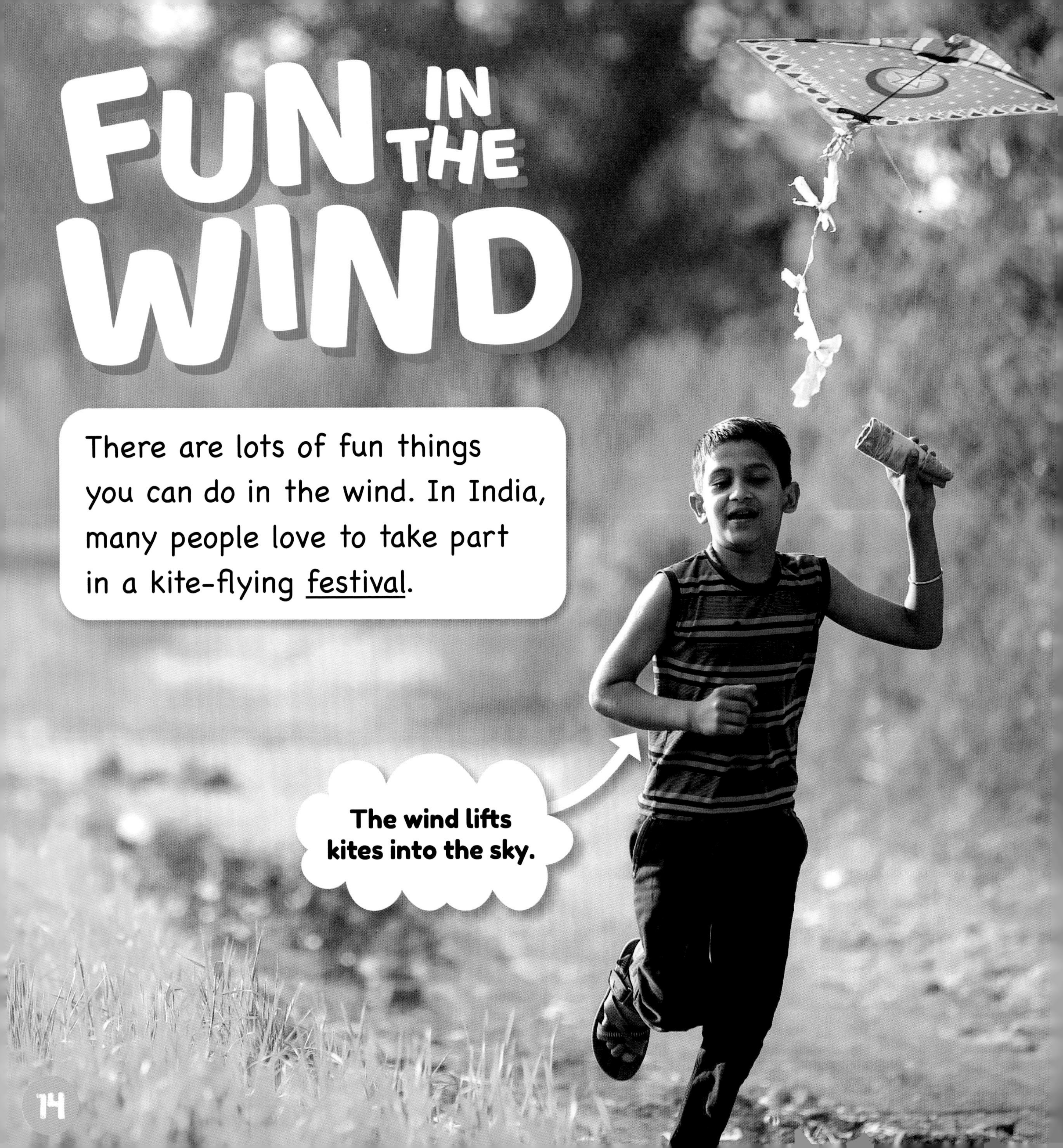

FUN IN THE WIND

There are lots of fun things you can do in the wind. In India, many people love to take part in a kite-flying festival.

The wind lifts kites into the sky.

Being safe when flying a kite is very important. Always fly a kite in an open, empty space. This will stop anyone getting hurt by the kite line.

PLANTS

When plants are seedlings, small breezes help them grow into stronger plants. However, sometimes a strong wind might damage plants by blowing them over.

These seedlings are growing into taller, stronger plants.

Wind also helps some plants by blowing their seeds everywhere. The seeds then settle in the soil and grow into new plants.

STORMS

A windstorm is a very strong wind that is moving quickly. Windstorms can even blow over big trees!

Oh no! The windstorm is blowing everything away!

Wind can also be part of other storms, such as thunderstorms and blizzards. Thunderstorms can sound scary but do not usually last too long.

EXTREME WIND

Tornadoes and hurricanes are types of extreme wind. A tornado is made of wind that moves very quickly in a tall column.

A hurricane is different from a tornado because it is much bigger and can last longer. Hurricanes can also be called typhoons or cyclones.

Did you know that hurricanes form over the oceans?

ANIMALS

Lots of animals, such as cats and dogs, need rescuing if they get stuck in extreme wind. Sometimes, animals in the wild lose all their food because the strong winds blow everything away.

These dogs are waiting to be rescued.

Burrowing owls hide away when the wind gets too strong.

Some animals find ways to protect themselves by burrowing deep into the ground and hiding away until the storm has passed.

GLOSSARY

blizzards	heavy snowstorms that last for a long time
breeze	a light or gentle wind
column	a tube shape, usually tall and thin
damage	to hurt or harm
extreme	when something is far beyond what is usual or normal
festival	an event where people get together to celebrate something
form	to make, build or create
seedlings	young trees or plants grown from a seed
temperature	how hot or cold something is

INDEX